AF270603

PISCES

by Elizabeth Andrews

popbooksonline.com/pisces

abdobooks.com

Published by Pop!, a division of ABDO, PO Box 398166, Minneapolis, Minnesota 55439. Copyright © 2026 by Abdo Consulting Group, Inc. International copyrights reserved in all countries. No part of this book may be reproduced in any form without written permission from the publisher. DiscoverRoo™ is a trademark and logo of Pop!.

Printed in the United States of America, North Mankato, Minnesota.
042025
082025

THIS BOOK CONTAINS RECYCLED MATERIALS

Cover Photo: Splendoura Prints; Shutterstock Images
Interior Photos: Alamy Stock Photo; Getty Images; Shutterstock Images
Editor: Tyler Gieseke
Series Designer: Laura Graphenteen

Library of Congress Control Number: 2024948392

Publisher's Cataloging-in-Publication Data
Names: Andrews, Elizabeth, author.
Title: Pisces / by Elizabeth Andrews
Description: Minneapolis, Minnesota : Pop!, 2026 | Series: Zodiac signs | Includes online resources and index
Identifiers: ISBN 9781098247935 (lib. bdg.) | ISBN 9781098248475 (ebook)
Subjects: LCSH: Pisces (Astrology)--Juvenile literature. | Fish (Astrology)--Juvenile literature. | Zodiac--Juvenile literature. | Astrology--Juvenile literature. | Astrology--Charts, diagrams, etc.--Juvenile literature.
Classification: DDC 133.52--dc23

*Scanning QR codes requires a web-enabled smart device with a QR code reader app and a camera.

TABLE OF CONTENTS

MEET THE PISCES!

Pisces is the twelfth and final sign of the zodiac. People born between February 19 and March 20 are Pisces. When people ask for your "star sign," they are likely asking for your sun sign. This is the zodiac sign the sun appeared in at your birth.

Water Lily

PISCES

constellation

feminine

aquamarine

mutable

numbers

2

6

FRI

symbol

ZODIAC CALENDAR

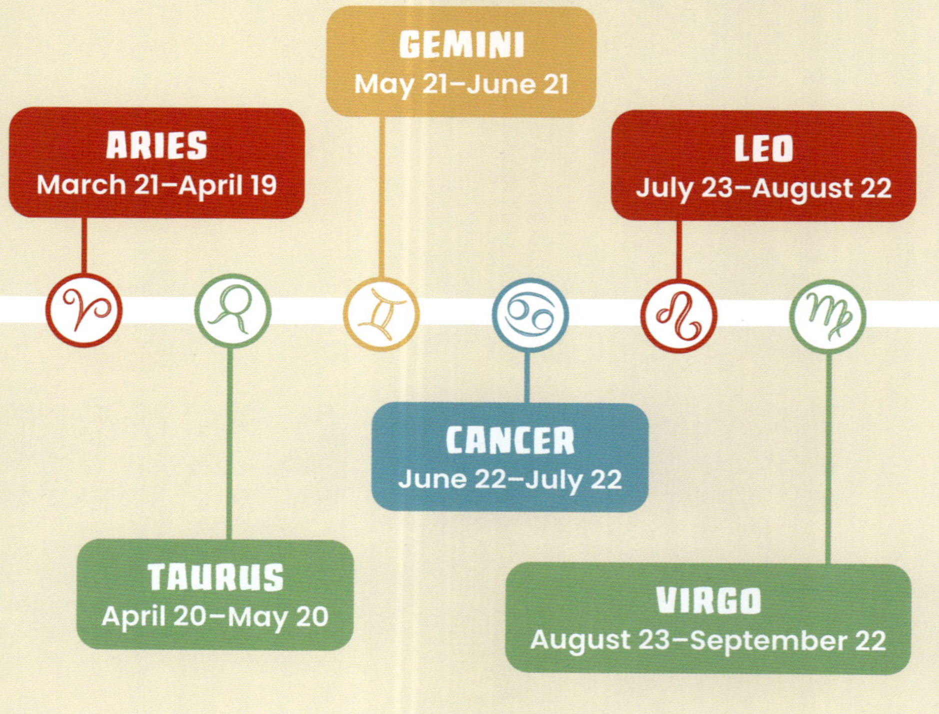

Three features help describe

zodiac signs. Signs can be masculine

or feminine. Each zodiac sign is given

a mode. The three modes are cardinal,

fixed, and mutable. Each zodiac is also

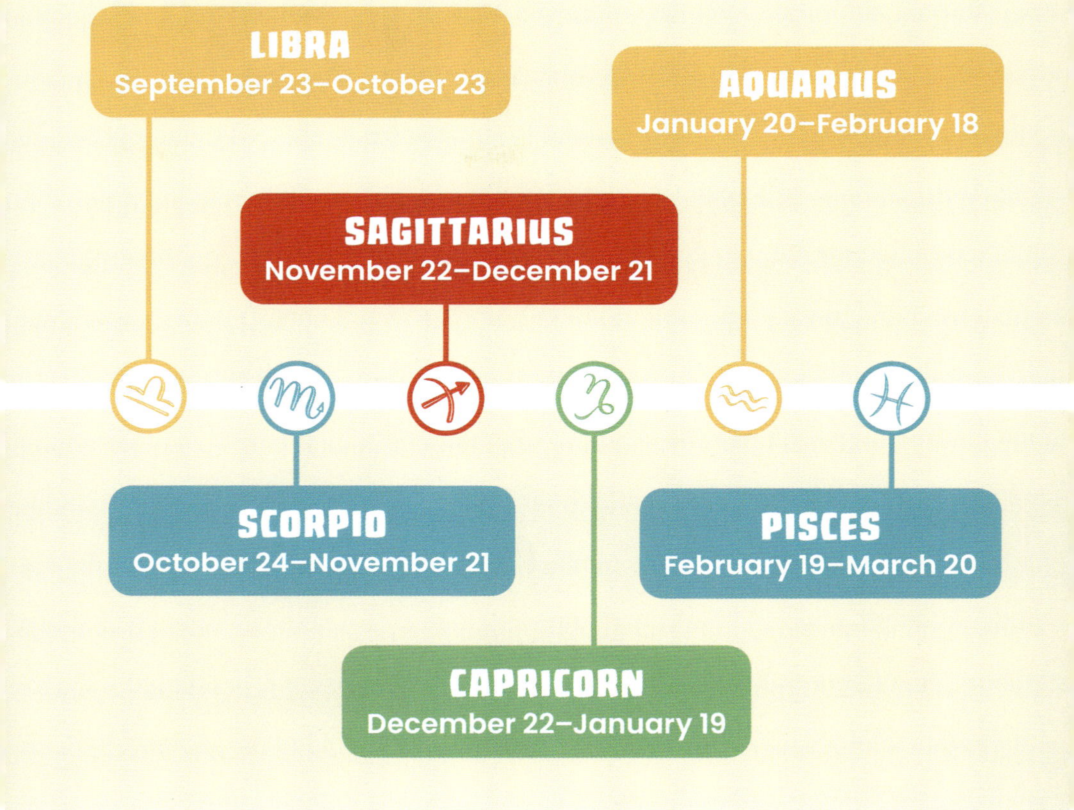

a fire, air, earth, or water sign. No zodiac sign shares the same three features.

DID YOU KNOW?

Pisces is the Latin word for "fishes."

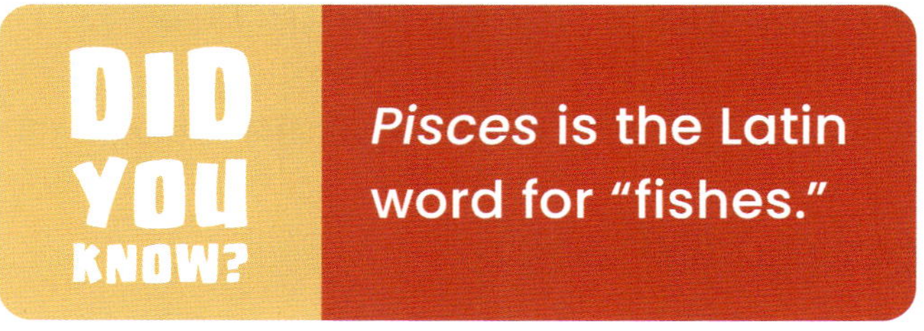

Pisces are good at understanding their friends' feelings.

Pisces is a feminine, mutable, water sign. Feminine signs are grounded. Many of their actions are done **internally**. They are in touch with their own emotions and those around them.

Modes describe how signs interact with the outside world. Mutable signs are open-minded and comfortable with change. They are usually easygoing. Water signs are emotional and observant. They are often **sentimental** and **sensitive**.

Water signs enjoy hearing others' stories.

Aphrodite (left) is the goddess of love and beauty.

Pisces is **represented** by two fish swimming in different directions. It is one of the oldest recorded zodiac signs. In ancient Greek mythology, Pisces represents the fish that the goddess Aphrodite and her son Eros turned into to escape an evil giant. Other stories say two fish freed Aphrodite and Eros and carried them to safety.

Eros (bottom) *shoots people with arrows to make them fall in love.*

HISTORY OF ASTROLOGY

Humans have looked for life's **spiritual** meaning since the beginning of time. They often looked to the stars for this. Astrology is the practice of reading the movements of planets and other **celestial** bodies and connecting them to life on Earth.

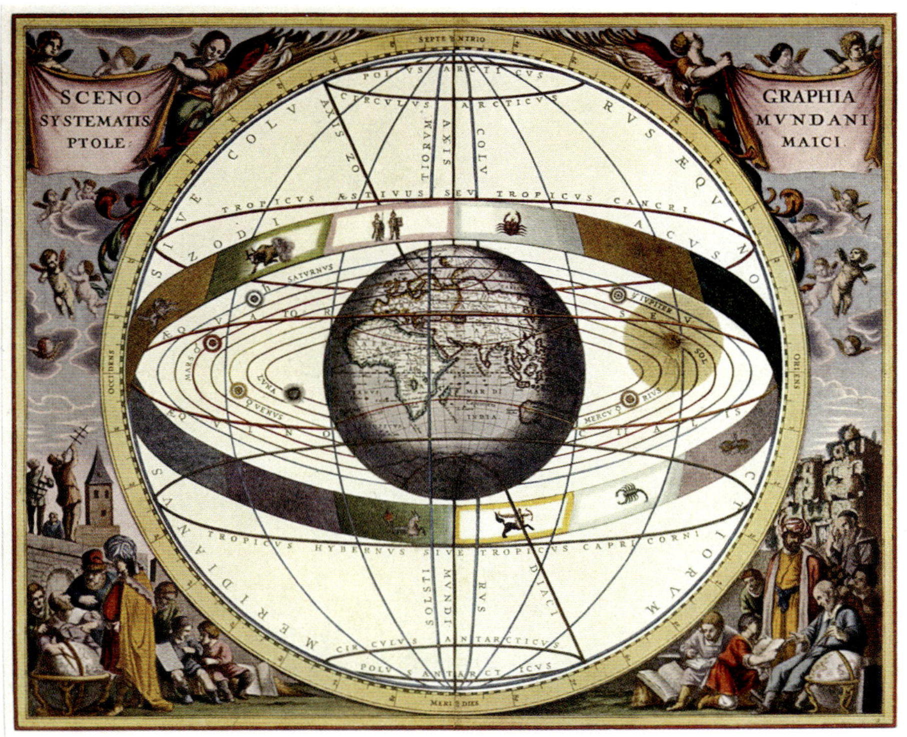

Some ancient people used the zodiac signs to predict future events.

Babylonians invented the zodiac in Mesopotamia over 5,000 years ago. Mesopotamia was the first known civilization. Babylon was one of the region's largest cities.

Ptolemy was an Egyptian man who studied the stars.

The zodiac is a belt of space around Earth that has 12 well-known **constellations**. Ancient people noticed that the sun seemed to move in front of these constellations throughout a year. The sun spends about a month in each constellation.

The constellations in the zodiac belt are Aries, Taurus, Gemini, Cancer, Leo, Virgo, Libra, Scorpius, Sagittarius, Capricornus, Aquarius, and Pisces. Together they make up the 12 zodiac signs. They are all **represented** by different **symbols**.

Islamic astrologers created new ways to map and measure stars.

THE ZODIAC WHEEL

DID YOU KNOW? Most zodiac symbols are animals. The ancient Greeks called the belt of space *zodiakos kyklos*, or "circle of animals."

THE SIGN OF DREAMS

Pisces are ruled by the planet Neptune. Neptune is named after the Roman god of the sea. This planet rules creativity, dreams, and mysteries. Some people describe Pisces as half body and half spirit. Often, Pisces feel pulled between the **spiritual** world and the real world.

DID YOU KNOW?

Of all the water signs, Pisces are the most **psychic**.

Pisces is the sign of dreams and imaginations. There is nothing Pisces enjoy as much as getting lost in their imaginations. They have a dreamy, childlike presence for their whole life. Pisces often prefer their dreams to their ordinary life. Pisces enjoy stories of magic and fantasy.

Pisces chase what makes them feel good. Often, they run away from anything too difficult or upsetting. Pisces see the world as what it can be. They want to believe good things happen. Pisces can use their imaginations and escape the hard world through creative art such as music, writing, or painting.

Amanda Gorman is a Pisces. She is known for her beautiful poetry.

Spending time outside can help Pisces connect with their creativity.

As a mutable water sign, Pisces go with the flow. They can be compared to ocean waves. Pisces must work to remain balanced and committed to what they need to get done. Like the sign of two fish **represents**, Pisces are often pulled between what they want to do and what they should do.

Pisces is best viewed between September and January.

FULL OF COMPASSION

Pisces is the final sign of the Zodiac. This means that Pisces have taken in all the lessons from the signs before them. Their qualities are a mix of those of all the zodiac signs. From day to day, a Pisces might be wild like an Aries or gentle like a Taurus.

Aquamarine is a soothing and peaceful stone.

Olivia Rodrigo
is a Pisces.
She writes
songs about
her emotions.

With all the lessons from the signs before them, Pisces are very compassionate. This means Pisces deeply understand other people's feelings. Sometimes they take on the feelings as their own. They will feel other people's joy, anger, and sadness. Compassion is Pisces' greatest strength and weakness, because they can get lost in all the emotions.

Pisces bring magic to the people they care about. They get very close to their friends and understand what makes them special. Pisces might also take people on as projects. Sometimes people will see how much Pisces are willing to do for others and take advantage of them. It is important for Pisces to choose friends wisely.

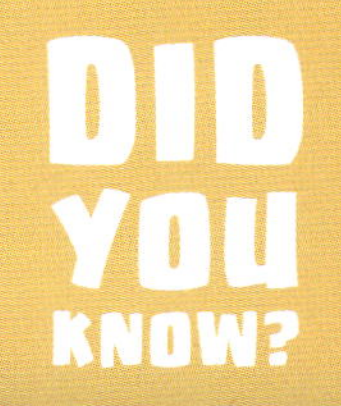

Pisces will take in sick plants and animals to care for them.

Pisces might enjoy working at animal shelters.

Pisces are very giving. They are drawn to work where they can help others. Pisces would do well in helping after natural disasters. They may also like getting involved in projects that let them explore new ideas and dreams. Pisces want to see the world become a better place.

Today, astrology can answer questions about an individual. People use astrology to understand who they are and why they might do what they do. It can also help them understand other people in their life. A zodiac sign can point out personal skills, possibilities, and **internal motivations**.

WHAT IS A BIRTH CHART?

Each person's birth chart contains all the planets in our solar system, the moon, and the sun. The location of where each **celestial** body was based on the exact time and location of a person's birth can be marked on a birth chart. A birth chart can explain even more about a person than what only a sun sign can. The placement of each planet affects the drive of a person. This reveals personal motivations. Astrology experts can read birth charts.

TEXT-TO-SELF

Are you a Pisces? If so, do you think the sign matches your personality? If not, what do you have in common with Pisces?

TEXT-TO-TEXT

Have you read any books about the other zodiac signs? How were those signs similar to and different from Pisces?

TEXT-TO-WORLD

With the help of an adult, look up famous Pisces. Pick one person and write a few sentences about ways that person shows Pisces qualities.

GLOSSARY

celestial — having to do with the sky or outer space.

constellation — a group of stars that forms a pattern.

internal — of, relating to, or being on the inside.

motivation — something that makes one want to do something.

psychic — having special mental abilities such as seeing the future or knowing others' thoughts.

represent — to stand for or be a sign of.

sensitive — feeling or noticing things quite sharply.

sentimental — causing or showing tender feelings.

spiritual — having to do with people's beliefs in things such as the soul, nature, and what happens after death.

symbol — an object or picture that represents something else.

INDEX

This book is filled with videos, puzzles, games, and more! Scan the QR codes* while you read, or visit the website below to make this book pop.

popbooksonline.com/pisces

*Scanning QR codes requires a web-enabled smart device with a QR code reader app and a camera.